Thank You

By buying this magazine, you support small business owners and small creators!

TalesOfTheGods aims to connect the metaphysical and spiritual communities.

Cover Photo - Mark Olsen on Unsplash.

If you would like to write in anonymously, or join our team for the next edition feel free to send a email to TalesOTheGods@gmail.com

TalesOfTheGods, March 2022

TalesOfTheGods.com

- PRACTICAL WITCHCRAFT -

facebook.com/groups/665578877692886

Contributors

Desirée Goulden	Owner, layout design, contributor
Kristian Heavenhill Maiorca	Photographer, Contributor
Dana Lee Beaudreau	Founding member, Contributor

The TalesOfTheGods & Practical Witchcraft magazine is a community project. Our roster of contributors is constantly shifting. Everyone who works on the magazine takes home an equal take of the income from the sales of this magazine.

We aim to bring education and entertainment to people of all levels of experience and paths. If you have a point of view that you would like to share with the world, feel free to reach out to join us. We are currently looking for people of colour to join us. Whether you are a teacher, or just interested in taking part, we have a place for you.

Have a shop or product you want to share with the world? Contact us and we will run a free full page ad for you in the next edition! We release on every day of the wheel of the year, so it's easy to follow release dates!

Please know that all opinions are that of the contributor and may not reflect the team in general.

Contents

About Ostara	PAGE 2
Cleansing Basics	PAGE 4
Hawthorn	PAGE 8
Unlocking Your Inner Magic	PAGE 10
Religious Sycronicities Not Religious Theft	PAGE 16
St Patrick's Day As a New Celtic Pagan	PAGE 20
Not So Proffesional Witches	PAGE 22

Jim Two Snakes
Spiritual Advisor

facebook.com/jimtwosnakes

instagram.com/jimtwosnakes

patreon.com/spiritualdad

Many people think the term Spirituality is about religion, but it doesn't have to be. In fact I think most people are Spiritual no matter if they are religious or not! Spirituality is about understanding and exploring your higher purpose, your interconnectedness to all of creation, and living authentically. It is my goal to help you feel inspired and fulfilled.

I do this by asking questions, giving suggestions, and then helping develop ways of marking progress and providing accountability. You don't have to believe the same way I, or anyone else, does. The coaching is centered around your needs and beliefs. I can't do the work for you, but I can help you with motivation and seeing things from a new perspective. Contact me now to schedule a free 15 minute initial consultation.

Ostara

Ostara is the 3rd on the Wheel Of The Year and marks the spring equinox. Ostara takes from the celebration of the Anglo-Saxon Goddess Ostara, or Esotre. Some say this is the time Persephone comes from the Underworld to help Demeter bring summer to the living world.

Christians celebrate Ester around this time, and throughout cultures this is a time of celebrating rebirth. The symbols for this day on the wheel of the year is the hare and the egg, and the colours for this day are soft greens, soft blues and yellows.

To celebrate you can begin planting your garden if your climate allows. You can clean and decorate your house (it's spring cleaning season soon anyway). You can take a walk through your local nature trail and clean any rubbish that you come across to honor the earth. You can chose to make up a special alter for the nature or fertility goddess of your choice. You can even decorate eggs like you would with your Christian family and friends.

The TalesOfTheGods & Practical Witchcraft magazine has hit its 1-year mark!

To celebrate we have released a hardback book containing every single edition from 2021!

https://www.talesofthegods.com/post/the-first-anniversary-special-edition-hardback-is-here

Cleansing Basics

One of the biggest things to understand for cleansing is that there are multiple layers to it. The basic summation of them would be physical, metaphysical, and emotional. At it's core with cleansing, you'll either be cleansing out the bad/stagnant/old/etc, but targeting a specific thing still, or or cleansing everything out (the good and the bad) to completely replace it all.

This means that you also want to think about that before you start your physical cleaning. I would caution against immediately going to dusting. Yes, please, don't forget to dust your house occasionally, but if you're goal with the cleaning is to mimic your metaphysical cleansing, tackling a doom pile or taking out the trash and tackling the laundry might actually be better. Essentially, you want to step back and look at it from the perspective of, "what area of my home right now needs to be tidied, organized, or cleaned to help the spiritual to stick?".

After the physical comes the metaphysical. Do your research on the different cleansing herbs and incenses since they all target different things and if you don't need to clear out the whole space, make sure the herb won't do that.

Beyond everything else on why don't use white sage if you're not in a practice that does so, is, it clears everything out the good and the bad. What happens when you clear out all the energy and don't replace it? A void. And voids either create more voids or get filled, so if you clear it all, fill it yourself.

There's also sound cleansing. So next time you're about to clean house, blast that music with intention to clean out the stagnant energy. Bells are also another lovely sound cleansing option. Yelling is also highly effective sometimes, arguably could have been one of the first sound cleansing methods used. Don't take that last statement too seriously, but imagine, suddenly you need to cleanse and have nothing on you and sound is not going to be an issue to your safety....

There's also the third layer to cleansing, that's just as important but forgotten, the emotional. You're not going to be able to filter out and work through everything thought/habit/emotion over night. That said, if you're cleansing after a breakup, a traumatic event, clearing out space for a new big life changes there will be thoughts and patterns that come up for you to basically sort through and keep what still fits and revamp or throw out what no longer does. Therapy, tarot, journaling, music, talking to a friend, meditation, etc, all very valid options for getting them to come up and getting started. On this end, the goal is to simply commit to baby steps you can actually hold yourself to.

This side of it is, yes, more of a preventative so to speak. Yes, an occasional cleansing will always be needed, but the goal when doing major cleansings should be to minimize the amount of work for the future.

Remembering all three and working them together will make your cleansings more impactful. .

—Kristian

SKILL SHare.

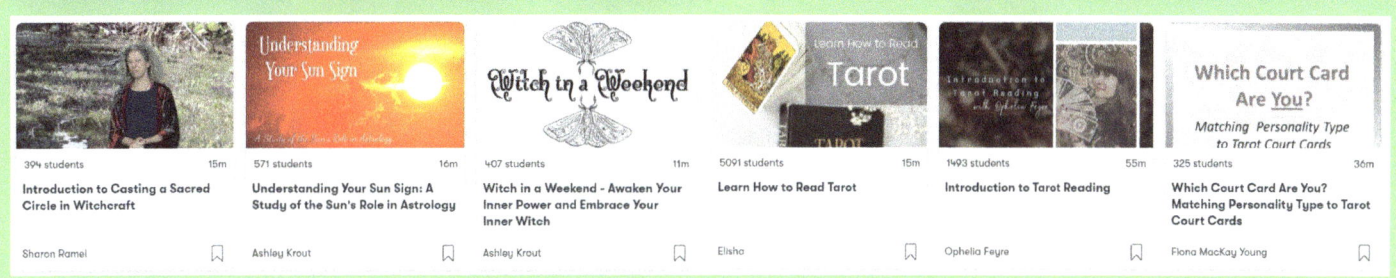

Want to learn more about your craft? Want to learn about the ins and outs of tarot and begin your path with professional teachers? Check out SkillShare!

SkillShare is an online learning community where you can learn everything under the sun from graphic design to the occult! Learn from professionals that provide engaging courses with projects that help you grow your craft and expand your knowledge.

Don't like commitment? Scan the QR code or enter the shortened link to get 1 free month of SkillShare on behalf of TOTG!

https://tinyurl.com/2p9xnn78

Hawthorn

Whether it be used in the manufacture of brooms, wands, warding garlands, or protection waters, Hawthorn has long been a staple in the witch's tool kit.

A member of the rose family, Hawthorn grows in temperate regions around the world. The leaves, bark, berries, flowers, stems, and even the roots can all be used in concocting natural medicines used for the heart, circulation, digestion, and kidneys. In identifying Hawthorn, the leaves look like little hands, the flowers are small and white, the berries are dark red, and the thorns are thick and spiky. Symbolically, Hawthorn is used to ward against harm, evil forces, and diseases. It is also used to remind us to love everyone that passes though our lives.

When harvesting Hawthorn, be sure to use a pair of thick gloves to avoid the sharp thorns. While these thorns are not poisonous, they are sharp enough to puncture the skin and require a tetanus shot. It may also be advisable to use gloves in the handling of the plant while you prepare your potions, tinctures, and warding crafts. The berries can be eaten raw or in a tea to boost immunity. The leaves and flowers are used to make the tea after they have been dried out in the sun.

While the branches are used in the making of broom stems, wands, door swags, and fairy houses (as fairies love to live among live Hawthorn, training your bush into a warm and inviting home for our lively neighbours will invite a co-harmonious existence between our two realms).

As simple as all this seems, others like myself may not be so adept at growing and harvesting this blessing of nature. A few tips for growing and harvesting it are:

- Be sure the seed is viable. This is done by dropping the seed in water. If the seed sinks, it's viable.

- Fill a small pot ¾ full with compost. Plant the seed. Cover and water but don't drown it.

- Leave the pot in a cool damp place. Outside over winter is optimal in order to push the seed.

- In spring the plant should begin to grow.

At this time, you can transplant it into the ground to grow until it's time to harvest it. They seem to prefer sun to light shade and high precipitation though efficient drainage is mandatory.

A classic to those who practice kitchen witchery, Hawthorn is indispensable even in modern times and in modern medicine.

-Dana

Unlocking Your Inner Magic

    I believe that most people possess some degree of giftedness and depending on the type or tenor, one may not be even aware of their full potential. Let me explain. Have you ever been stopped at a red light and suddenly felt that you should turn left instead of going straight and later hear that there was a major accident/ fire/ event on that route that you would have encountered? That would be the more common experience related by the average individual on the street. Sadly, I think this article may come off as a mish mash of disconnected ramblings because I have a lot to say and a tangled web of my own experience with magics to work through to say it.

    In the beginning, we are a miraculous ball of potential. We have access to all kinds of skills, talents, gifts, magics and experiences. I conscribe to the idea of the historical soul where you carry through all of your memories, gifts, talents and knowledge into the future life and build upon that base until you reach a life where you complete your purpose and receive the right to rest. I also believe that time is a wheel not a line and your may be experiencing things out of order as you travel this road. That being said, I also believe that every individual does possess the full range of their power upon their birth as it is one of the essential tools in their toolbox that they are outfitted with in order to fulfil their destiny.

The difficulty begins with the question, "should you bind your child's magic or should you let it develop naturally?" Neither answer is wrong. It's simply a matter of parenting choice. While I understand the parent/practitioner who chooses to bind their child's powers in order to keep them from misusing them, causing harm to others, or causing harm to themselves, I also understand the choice to leave the child unbound and try to harness and harvest their abilities to their full potential. If you choose to bind your child, at what point/age do you unbind them? When is it time to open up their channel? When do you recognise what gift/magic do they possess? And how do you recognise it? These are all very good questions. In the early 80s, psychology magazines began to explore these questions from interesting perspectives. It was no longer a race to see who could read the most playing cards correctly or what number am I thinking of (which I think was to keep the unschooled masses from panicking that magic might harm them because they didn't understand it. Unfortunately, it was relegated to the realm of parlour games and entertainment.) Among these studies and new directions came the fascination of the existence of ghosts, demons and other spirits. Do not mistake what I am saying here. These do exist and they do interact with us but another anomaly opened up and made its presence known. Children in prepuberty and adolescence began to manifest and report strange events. Poltergeists, voices, unexplained phenomena started to occur around individuals in this age bracket and yet they were totally unaware of how they were potentially the reactor causing these events. Scientists began to explore and experiment with the idea of this phenomena. Unfortunately, humanity's need for safety nets and fences left out a lot of the possible explanations and potential that this study opened up. Many individuals start to show evidence of the gifts that they will manifest as early as within the first hours of life. In the rare case, even in utero the gift may begin to make itself known. So, if you choose to bind your child's gifts, be aware that this does not mean that there will be no evidence, accidental events, or occurrence of a sidebar of said gift making itself known. When it does, you need to be prepared to help your child harness and train up their abilities. The problem with waiting to unbind their gift is the potential that a rebellious child will not only misuse their gift but could potentially not understand what is happening and not be willing to rationally learn what tools they now have at their disposal. Also, being late to the game, they may not be aware of all the ways that said tools can be used. In the event that you choose to leave your child's gifts unbound the pros and cons should also be considered. While you can help your child grow and develop their gift more gradually, you can also help them to bravely explore the unknown or untried possibilities that their gift may offer up. Much like any other science, what we know is never the end of the journey. New and untried doors may appear along life's hallway where you can -

pick and choose to open familiar or new ones as you go. When leaving your child unbound, you need to stay alert. Learning/teaching should occur on an almost continuous basis. Each person possesses unique gifts/magic so you should not create a judgemental or limited environment. (Personal note: this became very obvious to me in my own children and yet I didn't recognize it until my son was in his teens. He asked one question and I had no answer because it did not fit my own basket of experience. To this day I am still seeking out answers to the questions my children ask.) I am not foolish enough to expect that anyone ever reaches their full potential but that 1) studies show that children will learn 60% of everything they will learn in life before they reach 6 years of age, and 2) we should continue to learn and grow and explore the boundaries of our own gifts every minute of everyday until this segment of our journey has passed.

Your next question may be "How do I open up my child/myself to the full potential of these gifts/magics?" I was going to say simple, but it's probably not.

First, begin by inviting the individual, even if that is yourself, to create a vision board. A blind vision board is most effective.

Second, watch and observe for interests and attempts at passions in the day-to-day activities that occur. Then create opportunities to further explore these.

Third, in some cases, hypnosis, psychic surgery, or reiki can help open blocked channels which may corrode or get stuck due to disuse.

While all of this may seem confusing to some and commonplace to others, I am encouraged to share this last bit of incite with you. No matter when, how or who, the existence of magics in others should always be treated with respect and kindness. No one is more/less than any other. From aura reading, insight, mediumship, pyro gifts, kinetics, telepathy, kitchen witchery, or any other; magics are simply a miracle and a gift. It's how you approach it that changes the world it abides in.

-Dana

instacart

Not everyone has the time to go shopping, or the transportation to do so. Luckily Instacart has your back! Instacart is an app that delivers from participating retailers that matches you with a personal shopper who will deliver it right to your door. They keep in contact with you through the shopping session and can chat with you to make decisions and replacements when needed and you can track their journey to you on the app when they're done.

Save time and gas and have everything you need from printer ink to zucchini right to your door! Use the link https://inst.cr/t/cTNVZzVqZ2JN or scan the QR code to get $10 off your first purchase with Instacart!

Religious sycronicities not religious theft

 Every time a day on the wheel of the year passes witches seem to come out of the ground to claim that any Christian religion around that time of the year is directly stealing from "pagan" religions. You've heard people claim Yule is Celtic or Roman Saturnalia, Ostara is Easter, etc, etc. The problem is that when you actually look deeper there is often not much to support these claims, especially for Ostara. These are only two examples, but what people seem to forget when we talk about these things is historical religious synchronicities.

 There are the basics to consider like: the equinox is the equinox no matter what religion you are and is an astronomical event perceived on earth, people in the same area or hemisphere will have the same local flora, fauna, and animals give or take and thus will likely draw similar ideas about the symbology of such (think the rabbit being a symbol of fertility, acorn luck, and abundance, roses representing love or beauty to name a few). They may have gods and/ or entities that fulfill similar duties and thus celebrations of them can look similar.

This is just how religions and people work. There is only so much variance you can reasonably expect between them when we are all living on the same planet and experiencing more or less the same fundamental human experiences. This is why many people believe in archetypal gods across the world. Most cultures will have entities that watch over or control things like fertility, love, nature, the ocean, etc, and because of this it is very likely that they will look similar.

This idea that everything Christianity has is stolen from other religions is disingenuous and ignores that by that logic, so too has the Ancient Hellenic religion, the Ancient Roman religion, and the Kemetic religion, as well as all sects of Christianity and Abrahamic beliefs.

The reality of it is that when religions exist around each other (especially if they exist within the same general culture and nation) they tend to borrow from each other, collaborate, and emulate each other.

It is well known that the Ancient Greek religion is based on the Mycenaean and Minoan religions which preceded Ancient Greece by hundreds of years. It is well documented that Egyptian and Hellenic peoples mixed deities and traditions to the point where most Greek gods have an Egyptian and Sumerian (the predecessor for Christianity and Judaism) version. Not counterpart: version. These were openly regarded as the same deity back in their days. Jews borrowed from the Sumerians, Christians borrowed from Jews,

Islam borrowed from both Jews and Christians, Christians borrowed from their pagan surroundings because it formed in Rome, a place notorious for directly taking from Ancient Greeks and believing that to thrive (originally in its early days) you have to honor ALL the people's gods and traditions.

I understand that the Christians have done some pretty terrible things in recent history, and as the current ruling religious power in the west, we see them as some over ruling evil tyrant especially because many of us have religious trauma, but the idea that they stole all their traditions rubs me the wrong way. Their practices arrived the exact way that everyone else's has through history: by being influenced by others. The difference is that it was formed in an empire that weaponized religion to colonize much of the Ancient world, thus its attitudes, practices, and ways are influenced majorly by that colonist mentality.

Furthermore, it's crimes are not unique. The Jews historically were attacked and prosecuted by the Ancient Hellenic peoples (research Chanukah.) who were notorious for enslaving the people of other religions and places. For as long as religions have existed there have been similarities, synchronicities, and wars involved because religions were not as they are now. They were not just beliefs, they were communities, a joint people and culture that in many cases were the single thread of similarity and community that held together villages and families across the globe in an era that was not as well connected as we are today.

When I hear people claim that "Christianity stole our holiday!" I see someone who is looking for conflict and superiority rather than actual understanding. Christianity evolved as most other religions do, and while they have many things to answer for in recent years, "stealing holidays" is not one of them, and more often than not, when you look to back up these claims they fall short... which is not something the wheel of the year can say, but that is a topic for another day.

—Desiree

St Patrick's Day As a New Celtic Pagan

When I woke up that morning, my first st. Patrick's day following Brighid, I knew it was going to be different. The day felt tinged with an element of sorrow that no one else seemed to be conscious of. The snakes St. Patrick drove out.... Were real people with lives and a culture and religion that was almost all lost.... All because the Catholic Church...

We preach separation of church and state in the united states while embracing holidays that are rooted in religion. Everyone's a little Irish that day they say, as if that really justifies drinking to a genocide. As I sit there in my black for mourning and a red sashay to symbolize the lives lost, my pentacle on proud display.

I watched everyone around my drink while I spent a few moments in meditation with Brighid. Someone asked me where my green was that day, and I immediately felt the "am the villain?" vibe when I replied with, "I am dressed for the day. In mourning for my brothers and sisters.   .

The truth be told, I'm Irish Italian American, I have Celtic pagan ancestors and VERY catholic ancestors that might have helped with the slaughter. It was as much for them and to honour Brighid as it was a way for me to cope.

I don't know if this holiday will get harder or easier going forward as I step into the Celtic path more. I just knows I can't and I won't celebrate the holiday anymore, unless it's to mourn with Brighid.

-Kristian

Not so proffesional witches

There are many positives and negatives that have come with the witchy community moving online. More access to materials and books, more access to communities, more access to diverse practices and paths, and unfortunately more access to frauds and people just in it to take your money. For those of us who were on our path before the internet became as influential, we could generally tell who was a fraud or not depending on their amount of performance. If we wanted our cards read, we would do so ourselves or go to a local reader who we know has a history of good work or hangs around the local metaphysical shop. In general, we wouldn't go to the crazy lady on the street corner yelling that she can tell you whether or not you have cancer and directly connect you to Jesus.

The problem these days is that those red flags that would point out an obvious fraud 10 - 15 years ago is the kind of thing that gets you clout, followers, and business online now. Let me explain.

The internet has come a long way from what it used to be. It has gone from dial-up and AOL catfishing to mega-media corporations and -

-being involved in every aspect of our lives. As such, it has gone from a place where you can just reach out and be heard to a competition.

To get any sort of attention online you need to market yourself in some way or another. Instagram influencers use professional photoshop and filters, TikTok influencers use filters, music, effects, and video editing to appear as something they're not, Facebook people just make a group and lie and people seem to go along with it because Facebook is a lawless place. For all of these platforms if you look the part and lie with enough confidence you can grow a massive following of new and impressionable practitioners.

It has become evident (especially in recent years) that many new practitioners don't do the physical research required to move forward in their craft. They often expect to find information on Google and expect to be spoon-fed what they cant Google by "reputable" witchy content creators online. This was somewhat of a problem on Tumblr and Facebook, but since the pandemic TikTok and by extension, Witchtok has become the hub for witchy content, information, misinformation, legitimate creators, teachers, and frauds.

These newer practitioners turn to creators on these platforms for the main source of their information. They are dazzled by people with beautiful altars. By beautiful people who claim they are stronger than what they are, and that they (despite rarely being over 25) are some sort of priestess or priest or the-

-reincarnation of a deity and you can only learn to be a "real witch" if you follow them and buy their products and sign up for their patreon and join their discord where nobody can monitor what is being said and they can curate who joins.

This would be semi-permissible if these people were not themselves new practitioners with no real knowledge. Earlier this year I was contacted by a friend of mine to ask for help addressing a certain person who was selling spells on Etsy. Normally I keep my nose out of that sort of thing, but as she explained more about the situation I and a few others had to step in. This person was only a practicing witch for under a year, had a reasonable following on Facebook and TikTok and was selling spell bottles with animal skulls tied to them. These spells were not baneful workings either, these were prosperity workings, protections, blessings, and fertility workings.

This mixed with the fact that this person was trying to teach people on their platforms about magic made for a very worrying situation. Add the customers that sought out my friend about this person's failed spellwork making things terrible for them after buying, we had to address it.

My friend saw people try to talk to her about it before only to end up blocked and then attacked on social media and have their followers sent after them. My friend sent me in and talked me up and when I respectfully approached this person the truth came out: They had only been practicing for under a year, the skulls were purely for aesthetic, they didn't know and they proceeded to ask me about very basic fundamental cleansing and protections they could do that should be some of the first things they've learned.

This person could not do a simple cleansing, but they were selling fertility and prosperity workings on Etsy for exorbitant prices. Just this week I was talking to a different friend about a Witchtok influencer with thousands of followers selling hexwork to their followers. They would have my friend help them with the hexwork and also had her put up protections around her house. They have only been practicing for 9 months and constantly make videos regurgitating other more knowledgable people's content while pretending to constantly be under attack. The reality is that much like the other person mentioned here, they could barely perform simple wards. Much of the work they are selling is my friend's work and the moment she stopped helping them their videos turned to "omg I'm being cursed by so many people, I'm under attack, I'm a badass don't mess with me."

Nobody is cursing them, they don't have many enemies, the reality is that when they have to do their own hexwork which they are selling on Etsy, it is backfiring and they are receiving return-to-senders.

None of this is new, these are only two stories of a dozen or so from this year alone of people (primarily TikTokers and Etsy witches) who have no idea what they are doing, selling to people online who eat up-

-their content and shell out their money because the person in question is good at making videos and marketing themselves to people who don't know better.

If you go on Etsy right now you can see hundreds of "mediums" and "priestesses" selling things like "Direct connection to Hades soul contract guaranteed success" (an actual listing, not made up and pretty common) or protection workings that are bottle spells where you can actually see the ingredients inside aren't at all correlated to what the spell should be. Go to TikTok and big creators can't tell you the difference between the properties of lavender and mugwort, but they can totally give you a list of herbs to induce abortions that definitely won't kill you in the process. They'll manufacture witch wars and use the boisterous performance and vitriol to make videos about how they like really, really, really need your money guys because "excuse XYZ" and then sell tarot readings that are false for $15 a pop.

I am not saying that people shouldn't sell their wares online. People within the witchy community should be allowed to sell their services and we should support creators and practitioners of all levels and income, but we should absolutely be pointing out obvious frauds. While we more experienced people can point out dangerous or uneducated people trying to make a quick buck or start a cult, new practitioners who only learn online can't.

I believe that if we want to ensure the safety of a new generation of occult practitioners and pagans who lean towards occult practices, we need to openly point out dangerous figures. I believe that we need to direct people away from things like Discord where there is no public moderation and is completely controlled by these problematic creators. We need to have open discourse that does not result in doxxing, harassment, and kicking people off their platforms, but addresses the root of this problem: young people not having easy access to resources, and manipulative practitioners using that to make money and boost their ego.

The time where we can pretend like the internet is not a part of our communities has passed, and we can no longer stand on the sidelines and allow these people to continue to hurt others and themselves. There's a lot of things that we need to change and fix, but I believe the first thing we need to do is to fish out these not-so-professional professional witches and educate people on how to spot and avoid cult-like behavior and manipulation.

-Desiree

Photo Credits

Conscious Design

Edz Norton

Jean Beller

K Mitch Hodge

Kyrylo Kazachek

Lobostudio Hamburg

Maria Lin Kim

Matt Briney

Michal Balog

Petr Sidorov

Rhett Wesley

William Farlow

TalesOfTheGods.com

facebook.com/groups/665578877692886